Smart
Writing

1

영작문 기초 탄탄하게 잡아주는 Smart Writing 1

지은이 전종삼, 스티브 브라운, 조금배
펴낸이 안용백
펴낸곳 (주)넥서스

출판신고 1992년 4월 3일 제311-2002-2호 ①
121-893 서울시 마포구 양화로 8길 24
Tel (02)330-5500 Fax (02)330-5555

ISBN 979-11-5752-555-3 54740
    979-11-5752-554-6 (SET)

가격은 뒤표지에 있습니다.
잘못 만들어진 책은 구입처에서 바꾸어 드립니다.

본 책은 〈Writing Master 1〉의 개정판입니다.

www.nexusEDU.kr
NEXUS Edu는 (주)넥서스의 초·중·고 학습물 전문 브랜드입니다.

영작문 기초 **탄탄하게** 잡아주는

Smart
Writing

전종삼 · 스티브 브라운 · 조금배 지음

1

NEXUS Edu

지 은 이   소 개

전종삼
• 미국 뉴욕 주립대학교 영어교육학 석사
• 한양대학교 TESOL 수료

스티브 브라운
• 영국 증권 투자 위원회 학사
• 미국 앤도버 국제영어학교 TEFL 수료

조금배
• 미국 하와이 퍼시픽 대학교 TESL 석사
• 정이조영어학원 팀장

Introduction

Smart Writing is designed to help you become a better writer. It will teach you about the process of writing. The writing process consists of more than just picking up a pencil and writing a paragraph or an essay from beginning to end. Writing is a process because it goes through many stages. It starts with understanding what is expected of you in a writing assignment. Next, it involves thinking about what you are going to write and planning how you are going to organize it. The final steps involve writing, checking your work, and rewriting. Being a good writer means you continually change, add to, and improve what you have already written.

Sometimes the hardest part of writing is deciding what you are going to say. That is why the models in this book are organized around topics familiar to most people. While you are doing the prewriting activities and reading the models, you should think about the topic and how it relates to you and your life. Then, when it's your time to write, you will have some ideas about what you want to say.

In addition to organization, you will learn other aspects of writing, including punctuation, the use of linking words, and paragraph and essay formats. To become a better writer, you must start with the basics of format and organization.

There are so many people to thank when you write a book like this. Our family members have been very supportive of us. We are also very thankful for all the people giving us precious tips for this book. And, most of all we would like to thank our publisher 'NEXUS.'

We hope that you enjoy using this book and that it helps you improve your English.

Warm-up

- The "Picture Description" section gets students to look at a picture and answer some simple questions. Students are introduced to words and phrases used in the unit and gain insight into the unit topic.

- The "Building Vocabulary" section provides more words and phrases that are relevant to the unit topic. The words and phrases are used in context to ensure students know how to use them accurately.

Reading and Understanding & Complete the Outline

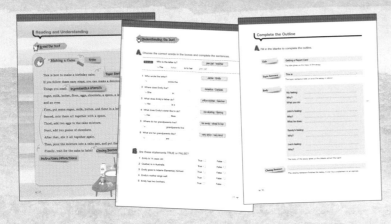

- Students read a passage about the topic in the "Read the Text" section. The passage contains examples of the grammar point that will be studied in the unit, and the passage is structured so that students can use it as a template for their own writing.

- The "Understanding the Text" section makes sure students fully comprehend and understand the passage.

- In "Complete the Outline," the students further reinforce their comprehension of the text and their understanding of the components of different types of writing: essays, letters, presentations, emails etc.

Grammar Point

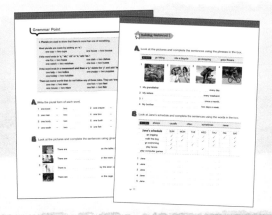

- The "Grammar Point" section explains the grammar topic of the unit. Students reinforce their knowledge of the grammar point via exercises.

- In "Building Sentences," students practice both the sentence structures used in the reading passage and the unit grammar point so that they are ready to write their own text.

Writing

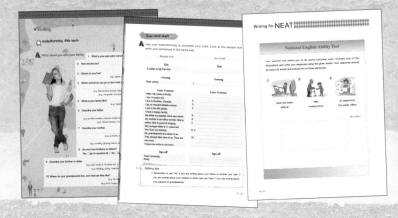

- The "Brainstorming" section guides students to find their own ideas to use in their writing task.

- In "Your First Draft," students use their brainstorming in a guided writing exercise that follows the structure and format of the reading passage.

- In "Writing for NEAT," students are given the opportunity to practice skills that will be needed in the National English Ability Tests.

Workbook

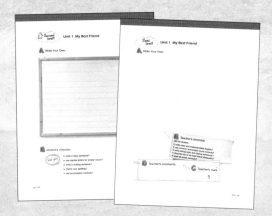

Students revise and edit their first draft, and produce a final draft of their writing task.

Students can write their final draft on their WORKBOOK.

* Answers download at www.nexusEDU.kr

Contents

Plan of the book

Unit 01

My Best Friend

My best friend is Gary James. Gary James is a boy. He is 13 years old. He wears glasses. He is from a country called England. His birthday is in July. Gary's hobby is riding his bike. His favorite drink is a milkshake. He has a pet bird called Harry. I like Gary James because he is very brave. I want to be his best friend forever.

Unit 01 My Best Friend

Warm-up

picture Description

A Look at the picture carefully and answer the questions.

| Example | Is the boy tall or short? ↘ He _____ is tall _____ . |

1 Is the boy fat or slim?   ↘ He _____.

2 Is the boy happy or sad?   ↘ He _____.

3 Is the boy from America or England? ↘ He _____.

B Look at the picture carefully. Are these statements TRUE or FALSE?

1 The boy is wearing a red shirt.   True ☐   False ☐

2 The boy is wearing glasses.   True ☐   False ☐

3 The boy is wearing blue jeans.   True ☐   False ☐

Building Vocabulary

A Match each word to the correct picture.

1 sneakers _____

2 gloves _____

3 sweater _____

4 glasses _____

5 T-shirt _____

6 blue jeans _____

ⓐ ⓑ ⓒ ⓓ ⓔ ⓕ

B Fill in the calendar.

1

Sun	Mon	Tue	Wed	Thu	Fri	Sat
1	2	3	4	5	6	7
8	9	10	11	12	13	14
15	16	17	18	19	20	21
22	23	24	25	26	27	28
29	30	31				

2

Sun	Mon	Tue	Wed	Thu	Fri	Sat
			1	2	3	4
5	6	7	8	9	10	11
12	13	14	15	16	17	18
19	20	21	22	23	24	25
26	27	28	29			

March

Sun	Mon	Tue	Wed	Thu	Fri	Sat
				1	2	3
4	5	6	7	8	9	10
11	12	13	14	15	16	17
18	19	20	21	22	23	24
25	26	27	28	29	30	31

April

Sun	Mon	Tue	Wed	Thu	Fri	Sat
1	2	3	4	5	6	7
8	9	10	11	12	13	14
15	16	17	18	19	20	21
22	23	24	25	26	27	28
29	30					

May

Sun	Mon	Tue	Wed	Thu	Fri	Sat
	1	2	3	4	5	
6	7	8	9	10	11	12
13	14	15	16	17	18	19
20	21	22	23	24	25	26
27	28	29	30	31		

3

Sun	Mon	Tue	Wed	Thu	Fri	Sat
					1	2
3	4	5	6	7	8	9
10	11	12	13	14	15	16
17	18	19	20	21	22	23
24	25	26	27	28	29	30

July

Sun	Mon	Tue	Wed	Thu	Fri	Sat
1	2	3	4	5	6	7
8	9	10	11	12	13	14
15	16	17	18	19	20	21
22	23	24	25	26	27	28
29	30	31				

4

Sun	Mon	Tue	Wed	Thu	Fri	Sat
			1	2	3	4
5	6	7	8	9	10	11
12	13	14	15	16	17	18
19	20	21	22	23	24	25
26	27	28	29	30	31	

5

Sun	Mon	Tue	Wed	Thu	Fri	Sat
						1
2	3	4	5	6	7	8
9	10	11	12	13	14	15
16	17	18	19	20	21	22
23	24	25	26	27	28	29
30						

October

Sun	Mon	Tue	Wed	Thu	Fri	Sat
	1	2	3	4	5	6
7	8	9	10	11	12	13
14	15	16	17	18	19	20
21	22	23	24	25	26	27
28	29	30	31			

6

Sun	Mon	Tue	Wed	Thu	Fri	Sat
				1	2	3
4	5	6	7	8	9	10
11	12	13	14	15	16	17
18	19	20	21	22	23	24
25	26	27	28	29	30	

December

Sun	Mon	Tue	Wed	Thu	Fri	Sat
						1
2	3	4	5	6	7	8
9	10	11	12	13	14	15
16	17	18	19	20	21	22
23	24	25	26	27	28	29
30	31					

Reading and Understanding

My Best Friend   Title

My best friend is Gary James.   Topic Sentence

Gary James is a boy. He is 13 years old.

He wears glasses. He is from a country called England.

His birthday is in July. Gary's hobby is riding his bike.

His favorite drink is a milkshake. He has a pet bird called Harry.

I like Gary James because he is very brave.

I want to be his best friend forever.   Closing Sentence

Body

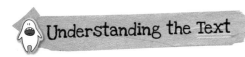
Understanding the Text

A Choose the correct words in the boxes and complete the sentences.

Example Who is Gary James?

| a girl / my teacher / my best friend |

↘ Gary James is _____my best friend_____.

---

1 What does Gary James wear?

| a cap / glasses / gloves |

↘ Gary James wears _____.

2 What is England?

| a city / a town / a country |

↘ England is _____.

3 What is a milkshake?

| a drink / a person / a hobby |

↘ A milkshake is _____.

4 What is Harry?

| a friend / a pet bird / a brother |

↘ Harry is _____.

5 What is Gary James like?

| kind / funny / brave |

↘ Gary James is very _____.

B Are these statements TRUE or FALSE?

1 Gary's best friend is Harry.   True ☐   False ☐

2 Gary was born in July.   True ☐   False ☐

3 Gary's hobby is drinking milkshakes.   True ☐   False ☐

4 Gary James is 13 years old.   True ☐   False ☐

5 I do not want to be Gary's friend.   True ☐   False ☐

Complete the Outline

 Fill in the blanks to complete the outline.

Title ----- My _____

: The title gives us the topic of the essay.

Topic Sentence ----- My best _____.

: The topic sentence gives us the main idea of the essay.

Body -----

About Gary James

Gender:	_____	boy / girl
Age:	_____	thirty / thirteen
Country:	_____	America / England
Birth Month:	_____	June / July
Hobby:	_____	bike / soccer
Favorite drink:	_____	juice / milkshake
Name of pet:	_____	Harry / Rover
Character:	_____	kind / brave

: The body of the essay gives us the details about the topic.

Closing Sentence ----- I want _____.

: The closing sentence finishes the essay. It can be a statement or an opinion.

Grammar Point

- **Common nouns** are a type of person, place, or thing.

girl	city	dog

Tip ◆ Common nouns do not begin with a capital letter unless they start a sentence.

- **Proper nouns** are the specific name of the person, place, or thing.

Emily	Seoul	Buster

Tip ◆ Proper nouns begin with a capital letter.

 Circle the common noun and underline the proper noun in each sentence.

Example   Gary James is a boy.

1   He is from a country called England.

2   He has a pet called Harry.

3   The Nile is a river.

4   September is a month.

5   My favorite drink is Coca-Cola.

 Write the following nouns in the correct box.

Word Box   China   Molly   city   Paris   country

                 cat   teacher   Coca-Cola   drink   Mrs. Lee

Common nouns

Proper nouns

13

 **Building Sentences 1**

 Match the phrases and write the sentences.

1 My best friend	•	ⓐ a pet dog called Rover.
2 She is	•	ⓑ a city called London.
3 She is from	•	ⓒ is Lucy.
4 Her hobby is	•	ⓓ twelve years old.
5 She has	•	ⓔ reading books.

1 _____

2 _____

3 _____

4 _____

5 _____

 Use the words in the boxes to complete the sentences. The words in the boxes may not be in the correct order.

The ___girl___ is my ___best friend___ .   best friend / girl

_____ is _____ of age.   she / 14 years

She _____ .   glasses / wears

Her _____ is in _____ .   November / birthday

Her _____ is playing _____ .   hobby / computer games

Her _____ food is _____ .   pizza / favorite

She has a _____ dog called _____ .   Butch / pet

She is a very _____ .   person / kind

I _____ to be her _____ forever.   want / friend

14

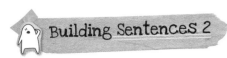

Building Sentences 2

 A Look at the pictures and complete the sentences using the words in the box.

Word Box	New York / city	China / country	Paris / city	Italy / country

1 She is from _____.

2 He is from _____.

3 She is from _____.

4 He is from _____.

 B Look at the pictures and complete the sentences using the phrases in the box.

A twenty years old	**B** twelve years old	**C** fifteen years old
jeans and a sweater	a blue dress	shorts and a T-shirt

1 The boy is _____.

He wears _____.

2 The woman is _____.

She wears _____.

3 The girl is _____.

She wears _____.

15

Writing

 Brainstorming ‹Pair Work›

A Write about your best friend.

1 What is your best friend's name? _____

2 Is your best friend a boy or a girl? _____

3 How old is he/she? _____

4 What does he/she usually wear? _____

> (e.g. glasses, jeans, a hat)

5 Where is he/she from? _____

> (e.g. a city called Beijing, a country called America)

6 Which month is his/her birthday in? _____

7 What is his/her hobby? _____

> (e.g. reading, singing, baseball)

8 What is his/her favorite food or drink? _____

> (e.g. ice cream, pizza, cola)

9 Does he/she have any pets?   Yes ☐ (go to question 10)

No ☐ (go to question 12)

10 If he/she has a pet, what kind is it? _____

> (e.g. dog, cat, fish, lizard)

11 What is his/her pet's name? _____

12 What is your friend's personality? _____

> (e.g. kind, brave, funny, friendly, clever, smart)

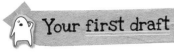
Your first draft

A Use your brainstorming to complete your draft. Look at the sample text and write your sentences in the same way.

Sample Text	Your Draft
Title	**Title**
My Best Friend	
Topic Sentence	**Topic Sentence**
My best friend is Gary James.	1.
Body	**Body**
Gary James is a boy.	2.
He is 13 years old.	3.
He wears glasses.	4.
He is from a country called England.	5.
His birthday is in July.	6.
Gary's hobby is riding his bike.	7.
His favorite drink is a milkshake.	
He has a pet bird called Harry.	8.
I like Gary James because he is very brave.	9, 10, 11.
	12.
Closing Sentence	**Closing Sentence**
I want to be his best friend forever.	

Editing tips

- If your friend is a boy, use "he/his." If your friend is a girl, use "she/her."
- Remember to begin a proper noun with a capital letter.
- Don't use a capital letter for a common noun unless it starts a sentence.

National English Ability Test

One of your friends invited you to his birthday party. However, you can't make it, so you have to refuse the invitation. Choose one of the illustrations and write your response using the given words. Your response should be about 20 words and include two or three sentences.

① take care of
home

② do my homework
tonight

③ visit my grandparents' house
sick

Word Count

Unit

02

Making a Cake

This is how to make a birthday cake. If you follow these easy steps, you can make a delicious cake. Things you need: sugar, milk, butter, flour, eggs, chocolate, a spoon, a bowl, a cake pan, and an oven First, put some sugar, milk, butter, and flour in a bowl. Second, mix them all together with a spoon. Third, add two eggs to the cake mixture. Next, add two pieces of chocolate. After that, stir it all together again. Then, pour the mixture into a cake pan, and put the pan in the oven. Finally, wait for the cake to bake!

Making a Cake

Warm-up

 Picture Description

A Look at the picture carefully. Match the phrases to make correct sentences.

1 The cake is •   ⓐ five candles.

2 The cake has •   ⓑ a birthday party.

3 The cake is for •   ⓒ white.

B Look at the picture carefully and choose the correct words in the boxes.

Example   There is a   (cake) / cakes .

1 There is a   girl / girls .

2 There are six   balloon / balloons .

3 There are three   present / presents   on the floor.

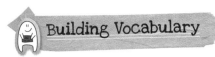

Building Vocabulary

A Match each word to the correct picture.

1 frying pan _____

2 kettle _____

3 bowl _____

4 oven _____

5 spoon _____

6 chopsticks _____

ⓐ ⓑ ⓒ ⓓ ⓔ ⓕ

B Look at the pictures and fill in the blanks using the words in the box.

Word Box	fry	add	bake	mix	boil	cut

1 _____ some sugar

2 _____ eggs and milk

3 _____ carrots

4 _____ some water

5 _____ vegetables

6 _____ some cookies

Reading and Understanding

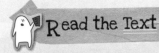 **R**ead the **T**ext

 Making a Cake **Title**

This is how to make a birthday cake. **Topic Sentence**

If you follow these easy steps, you can make a delicious cake.

Things you need: **Ingredients & Utensils**

sugar, milk, butter, flour, eggs, chocolate, a spoon, a bowl, a cake pan,

and an oven

First, put some sugar, milk, butter, and flour in a bowl.

Second, mix them all together with a spoon.

Third, add two eggs to the cake mixture.

Next, add two pieces of chocolate.

After that, stir it all together again.

Then, pour the mixture into a cake pan, and put the pan in the oven.

Finally, wait for the cake to bake! **Closing Sentence**

Instructions [=Directions]

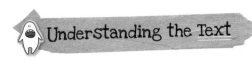

A Choose the correct words in the boxes and complete the sentences.

1 What are these instructions for?

↳ These instructions tell you how to make _____.

> a cake / a pie

2 What will you use to mix all the ingredients?

↳ I will use _____ to mix all the ingredients.

> an oven / a spoon

3 How many eggs do you need?

↳ I need _____ eggs.

> two / four

4 Where will you put the mixture?

↳ I will put the mixture into _____.

> a bowl / a cake pan

5 How much chocolate do you need?

↳ I need _____ of chocolate.

> two pieces / a bar

B Are these statements TRUE or FALSE?

1 If you follow the instructions, you can make a cake easily.   True ☐   False ☐

2 At first, you should put flour and salt in a bowl.   True ☐   False ☐

3 You don't need any water to make a cake.   True ☐   False ☐

4 You should mix all ingredients together before putting the mixture into a cake pan.   True ☐   False ☐

5 You should wait for the cake to boil.   True ☐   False ☐

Complete the Outline

 Fill in the blanks to complete the outline.

Title ┄┄┄┄ Making _____

: The title gives us the topic of the instructions.

Topic Sentence ┄┄┄ This is _____.

: The topic sentence tells us what the instructions are about.

Ingredients & Utensils ┄┄┄ Things you need: _____

_____

Instructions ┄┄┄

= steps to make a cake

First step: _____

Second step: _____

Third step: _____

Fourth step: _____

Fifth step: _____

Sixth step: _____

_____

: Instructions tell us how to do something.

Closing Sentence ┄┄ Finally, _____!

: The closing sentence finishes the instructions.

Grammar Point

● **Countable nouns** can be counted.

a book (singular) / two books (plural)
an apple (singular) / four apples (plural)
one foot (singular) / two feet (plural)

Tip◆ Countable nouns can be singular or plural.
They have "a/an" or a number in front of them.

● **Uncountable nouns** cannot be counted.

sugar, homework, luggage, money, water,
love, music, bread, news, furniture, rain

Tip◆ Uncountable nouns often have words such as
"much" or "little" in front of them, but do not
have a number in front of them.

A Decide whether the underlined noun is countable or uncountable.

1 I have good news.　　　　　　　　　Countable ☐　　Uncountable ☐

2 I like to play in a park.　　　　　　　Countable ☐　　Uncountable ☐

3 I want to eat two pears.　　　　　　Countable ☐　　Uncountable ☐

4 I like to play with a cat.　　　　　　Countable ☐　　Uncountable ☐

5 There is a lot of rain today.　　　　Countable ☐　　Uncountable ☐

6 Can I drink lots of juice please?　　Countable ☐　　Uncountable ☐

7 How much money do you have?　　Countable ☐　　Uncountable ☐

B Circle the uncountable nouns.

1　　　　　　2　　　　　　3　　　　　　4

5　　　　　　6　　　　　　7　　　　　　8

Building Sentences 1

A Complete the sentences using the words in the box.

Word Box	after that	add	mash	first
	next	drain	enjoy	boil

This is how to make mashed potatoes.

1 _____ , put some potatoes into a pot.

2 Second, _____ salt and water.

3 Third, _____ it for 20 minutes.

4 Fourth, _____ water from the potatoes.

5 _____ , put the hot potatoes into a bowl.

6 _____ _____ , add cream, butter, and pepper.

7 Then, _____ the potatoes.

8 Lastly, _____ it.

B Look at the pictures and unscramble the sentences.

1

(boil / water / some)

↳ _____

2

(in / a cup / put / a teabag)

↳ _____

3

(the hot water / into / the cup / pour)

↳ _____

4

(your / enjoy / cup of tea)

↳ _____

A Look at the pictures and complete the sentences using the phrases in the box.

Word Box	cut cucumbers	fry eggs	peel an orange
	grill chickens	stir coffee	spread butter

1
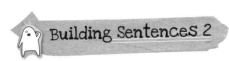
I _____ .

2
I _____ .

3
I _____ .

4
I _____ .

5
I _____ .

6
I _____ .

B Look at the pictures and complete the sentences using the given words.

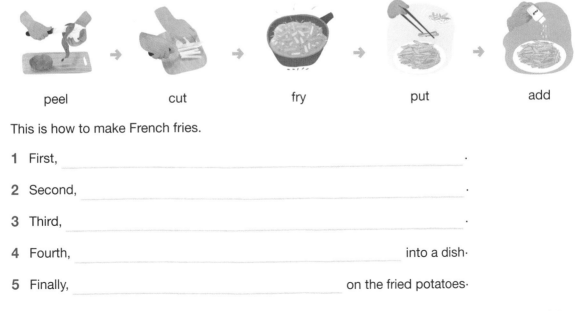

peel   cut   fry   put   add

This is how to make French fries.

1 First, _____ .

2 Second, _____ .

3 Third, _____ .

4 Fourth, _____ into a dish·

5 Finally, _____ on the fried potatoes·

27

Writing

 A Write some instructions for making something to eat.

1 What will you make?

_____

(e.g. a cake, a pizza, a sandwich)

2 What ingredients do you need?

_____

(e.g. bread, milk, cheese, vegetables)

3 What utensils do you need?

_____

(e.g. a kettle, a scoop, a knife, a pot)

4 What do you do with them first?

_____

(e.g. cut, boil, bake, fry)

5 What do you do with them second?

_____

(e.g. boil, bake, fry, mix)

6 What do you do with them third?

_____

(e.g. boil, bake, fry, mix)

7 What do you do with them next?

_____

(e.g. boil, bake, fry, mix)

8 What do you do with them after that?

_____

(e.g. boil, bake, fry, drop)

A Use your brainstorming to complete your draft. Look at the sample text and write your sentences in the same way.

Sample Text	Your Draft
Title	**Title**
Making a Cake	
Topic Sentence	**Topic Sentence**
This is how to make a birthday cake.	
Body	**Body**
If you follow these easy steps, you can make a delicious cake.	1.
Things you need: sugar, milk, butter, flour, eggs, chocolate, a spoon, a bowl, a cake pan, and an oven	2, 3.
First, put some sugar, milk, butter and flour in a bowl.	4.
Second, mix them all together with a spoon.	5.
Third, add two eggs to the cake mixture. Next, add two pieces of chocolate.	6.
After that, stir it all together again. Then, pour the mixture into a cake pan, and put the pan in the oven.	7.
Closing Sentence	**Closing Sentence**
Finally, wait for the cake to bake!	8.

Editing tips
- Remember that a countable noun can be counted, and it has "a/an" or a number in front of it.
- Remember that an uncountable noun cannot be counted, and it does not have "a/an" or a number in front of it.

National English Ability Test

Look at the picture carefully and describe what the people are doing.

There are some people in the park.

A tall boy _____(1)_____.

A girl with a doll _____,(2)_____.

A boy with red hair _____(3)_____.

A boy with a blue cap _____(4)_____.

Word Count

(1)

(2)

(3)

(4)

A Letter to My Pen Pal

Dear Jamie, Hello. My name is Emily. I am 14 years old. I live in Quebec, Canada. I go to Howard Middle School. I am in the 9th grade. I have a happy family. My father is a teacher. He is very clever. My mother is an office worker. She is pretty. She is good at singing. My younger sister is 11 years old. She likes ice-skating. My grandparents live close to us. They always take care of us. They are very kind. I hope you write to me soon. Yours sincerely, Emily

Unit 03 My New Pen Pal

Warm-up

Picture Description

A Look at the picture carefully and choose the correct words in the boxes.

| **Example** | Who is the prettiest in the family? ↘ My (mother) / father is the prettiest. |

1 Who is the tallest in the family?   ↘ My grandfather / father is the tallest.

2 Who is the youngest in the family?   ↘ My brother / sister is the youngest.

3 Who are the oldest in the family?   ↘ My parents / grandparents are the oldest.

B Look at the picture carefully. Are these statements TRUE or FALSE?

1 There are six people in my family.   True ☐   False ☐

2 Only my grandfather wears glasses.   True ☐   False ☐

3 My grandmother has short hair.   True ☐   False ☐

A Match each word to the correct picture.

1 **designer** _____

2 **police officer** _____

3 **firefighter** _____

4 **cook** _____

5 **pilot** _____

6 **office worker** _____

B Match each picture to the correct word.

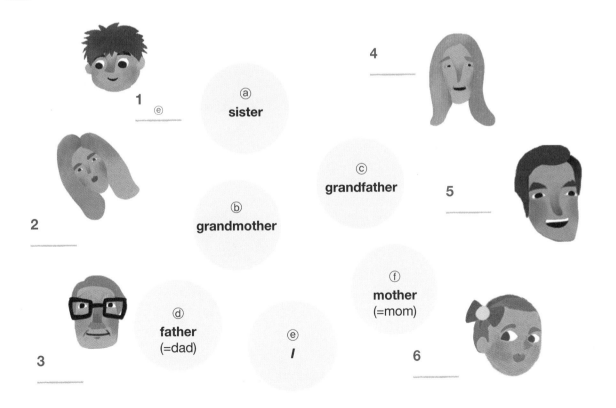

ⓐ **sister**

ⓑ **grandmother**

ⓒ **grandfather**

ⓓ **father** (=dad)

ⓔ **I**

ⓕ **mother** (=mom)

Reading and Understanding

 A Letter to My Pen Pal   **Title**

Dear Jamie,   **Greeting**

Hello. My name is Emily.

I am 14 years old. I live in Quebec, Canada.

I go to Howard Middle School. I am in the 9th grade.

I have a happy family. My father is a teacher. He is very clever.

My mother is an office worker. She is pretty. She is good at singing.

My younger sister is 11 years old. She likes ice-skating.

My grandparents live close to us. They always take care of us.

They are very kind.

Letter Contents

I hope you write to me soon.

Yours sincerely,   **Signoff**

Emily

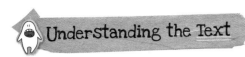

Understanding the Text

A Choose the correct words in the boxes and complete the sentences.

> **Example**   Who is the letter to?   pen pal / teacher
>
> ↘ The _____letter_____ is to her _____pen pal_____ .

1 Who wrote the letter?

> ↘ _____ wrote the _____ .

Jamie / Emily

2 Where does Emily live?

> ↘ She _____ in _____ .

America / Canada

3 What does Emily's father do?

> ↘ Her _____ is a _____ .

office worker / teacher

4 What does Emily's sister like to do?

> ↘ Her _____ likes _____ .

ice-skating / fishing

5 Where do her grandparents live?

> ↘ _____ grandparents live _____ .

far away / close to her

6 What are her grandparents like?

> ↘ _____ are _____ .

very strict / very kind

B Are these statements TRUE or FALSE?

1 Emily is 14 years old.   True ☐   False ☐

2 Quebec is in Australia.   True ☐   False ☐

3 Emily goes to Adams Elementary School.   True ☐   False ☐

4 Emily's mother sings well.   True ☐   False ☐

5 Emily has two brothers.   True ☐   False ☐

Complete the Outline

 Fill in the blanks to complete the outline.

Title

A _____

: The title gives us the topic of the letter.

Greeting

Dear _____ ,

: The greeting is the way to say hello to the person you are writing to.

Letter Contents

Emily's Age: _____

Where Emily Lives: _____

Emily's School: _____

Emily's Grade: _____

Her Father's Job: _____

Her Father's Personality: _____

Her Mother's Job: _____

Her Mother's Talent: _____

Her Sister's Age: _____

Her Sister's Hobby: _____

Her Grandparents' Home: _____

Her Grandparents' Personality: _____

: The letter contents give us the details of what you want to write about.

Sign-off

Yours _____ ,

_____ (Writer's Name)

: The sign-off is the way to say goodbye to the person you are writing to.

Grammar Point

Pronouns can be used instead of nouns, and personal pronouns can be used instead of nouns that are people or things.

	for people						for things	
Subjective	I	you	he	she	we	they	it	they
Possessive	my	your	his	her	our	their	its	their
Objective	me	you	him	her	us	them	it	them

 Circle all the personal pronouns in the text.

Hello. My name is Emily. I am 14 years old. I live in Quebec, Canada. I go to Howard Middle School. I am in the 9th grade. I have a happy family. My father is a teacher. He is very clever. My mother is an office worker. She is pretty. She is good at singing. My younger sister is 11 years old. She likes ice-skating. My grandparents live close to us. They always take care of us. They are very kind.

I hope you write to me soon.

 Choose the correct pronouns to complete the sentences.

1 I really like my grandparents. He / She / They like me, too!

2 My parents are great. He / I / They love them very much.

3 My sister plays volleyball. Her / She / They is very good at it.

4 I have five brothers. They / Them / I all like computer games.

5 Watch out! Us / Me / You must be more careful!

Building Sentences 1

A Put the given words in the correct order to complete the sentences.

Example	my / John / is / name	↘ Hello, _my name is John_ .

1 Elementary / to / School / New York ↘ I go _____ .

2 a / mother / doctor / is ↘ My _____ .

3 a / family / happy / are ↘ We _____ .

4 away / from / us / far / live ↘ They _____ .

B Look at the example and complete the sentences using pronouns and the given information.

Example My mom is a doctor.

↘ ___She___ is ___very___ ___caring___ .

> very caring

1 My brother is a university student.

↘ _____ _____ is _____ .

> major, math

2 My mother has a shop.

↘ _____ is _____ _____ _____ .

> a shop owner

3 My parents enjoy climbing and hiking.

↘ _____ like _____ .

> mountains

4 My sister enjoys songs and concerts.

↘ _____ likes _____ .

> music

5 My father likes exercising.

↘ _____ is _____ _____ .

> very healthy

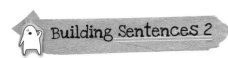

A Look at the pictures and complete the sentences like the example.

Example

There are _____ four people _____ in my family.

I have ____ a father, a mother, and a twin sister ____.

1

There are _____ in my family.

I have _____.

2

There are _____ in my family.

I have _____.

3

There are _____ in my family.

I have _____.

B Correct the mistakes and rewrite the sentences.

1 I want to tell you about me family.

↳ _____

2 My father is a writer. Him writes many books.

↳ _____

3 My younger sister is ten years old. Her likes painting.

↳ _____

4 My grandparents are very kind. I really like they.

↳ _____

Writing

A Write about you and your family.

1 What is your pen pal's name? _____

2 How old are you? _____
(e.g. 10 years old)

3 Where do you live? _____
(e.g. Japan, China, Greece, Germany)

4 Which school do you go to and what grade are you in?
_____
(e.g. Elementary School, Middle School, High School)
(e.g. 1st grade, 2nd grade, 3rd grade, 4th grade)

5 What is your family like? _____
(e.g. happy, close, big, small, funny)

6 Describe your father.
_____
(e.g. an office worker, a lawyer, a teacher, a policeman, a bank teller)
(e.g. clever, serious, kind, generous, gentle, funny)

7 Describe your mother.
_____
(e.g. a doctor, a shop worker, a housewife)
(e.g. pretty, slim, tall, short)
(e.g. cooking, playing tennis, playing the guitar, swimming)

8 Do you have brothers or sisters?
Yes ☐ (go to question 9) / No ☐ (go to question 10)

9 Describe your brother or sister.
(e.g. older sister is 16 years old, younger brother is 8 years old)
(e.g. reading, skiing, watching movies, listening to music)

10 Where do your grandparents live, and what are they like?
(e.g. far away, close to us, near, next to)
(e.g. kind, happy, caring, sweet, warm-hearted)

Your first draft

A Use your brainstorming to complete your draft. Look at the sample text and write your sentences in the same way.

Sample Text

Title

A Letter to My Pen Pal

Greeting

Dear Jamie,

Letter Contents

Hello. My name is Emily.
I am 14 years old.
I live in Quebec, Canada.
I go to Howard Middle school.
I am in the 9th grade.
I have a happy family.
My father is a teacher. He is very clever.
My mother is an office worker. She is pretty. She is good at singing.
My younger sister is 11 years old.
She likes ice-skating.
My grandparents live close to us.
They always take care of us. They are very kind.
I hope you write to me soon.

Sign-off

Yours sincerely,
Emily

Your Draft

Title

_____

Greeting

1. _____

Letter Contents

2. _____
3. _____
4. _____

5. _____
6. _____
7. _____

8, 9. _____

10. _____

Sign-off

_____
_____

Editing tips

- Remember to use "he" if you are writing about your father or brother, use "she" if you are writing about your mother or sister, and use "they" if you are writing about your parents or grandparents.

National English Ability Test

Your pen pal, David Smith, sent you an email. He asked a question about your favorite movie. Write a reply to your friend. (about 30 words)

Subject : my favorite movie-*Ghostbusters*

Hi, David.

_____

_____

_____

_____

_____

Susie

Word Count

Unit 04
My Birthday Party

Today is my birthday. I am at my birthday party. My friends are here. We are playing games. We are all laughing, talking, and singing. My mom made a delicious birthday cake. I want to eat it now. But first, I have to blow out the candles and make a wish. I also want to open my presents! My birthday party is fun!

My Birthday Party!

Warm-up

 Picture Description

A Look at the picture carefully and answer the questions.

| **Example** | Are they boys or girls? | ↘ They are _____girls_____ . |

1 Are they laughing or crying?   ↘ They are _____ .

2 Is she drinking or eating cake?   ↘ She is _____ .

3 Are they sitting around the table or standing up?   ↘ They are _____ .

B Look at the picture carefully. Are these statements TRUE or FALSE?

1 The children are happy.   True ☐   False ☐

2 There are candles on the cake.   True ☐   False ☐

3 There are four birthday presents.   True ☐   False ☐

Building Vocabulary

A Match each word to the correct picture.

1 make a wish _____

2 blow out _____

3 present _____

4 have fun _____

5 candle _____

6 balloon _____

B Match each picture to the correct word.

1 _____

2 _____

ⓐ **wedding**

ⓓ **graduation**

ⓑ **picnic**

ⓔ **funeral**

ⓒ **birthday**

4 _____

5 _____

3 _____

Read the Text

My Birthday Party   **Title**

Today is my birthday.   **Topic Sentence**

I am at my birthday party. My friends are here. We are playing

games. We are all laughing, talking, and singing.

My mom made a delicious birthday cake. I want to eat it now. But

first, I have to blow out the candles and make a wish. I also want

to open my presents!

Body

My birthday party is fun!   **Closing Sentence**

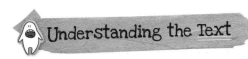

A Choose the correct words in the boxes and complete the sentences.

Example   What special day is today?

day / holiday / birthday

↘ Today is my _____birthday_____ .

1 Where are you?

school / birthday party / room

↘ I am at my _____ .

2 What are you and your friends doing?

making a cake / talking to my mom / playing games

↘ We are _____ .

3 What do you want to do to your cake?

eat / blow / drink

↘ I want to _____ my birthday cake.

4 What do you have to do first?

go home / blow out the candles / see my mom

↘ First, I have to _____ .

5 What do you also want to do?

open my presents / play games / blow up a balloon

↘ I also want to _____ .

B Are these statements TRUE or FALSE?

1 Yesterday was my birthday.   True ☐   False ☐

2 We are singing at the party.   True ☐   False ☐

3 My sister made me a cake.   True ☐   False ☐

4 I opened my presents and really liked them.   True ☐   False ☐

5 We are having a good time at the party.   True ☐   False ☐

Complete the Outline

 Fill in the blanks to complete the outline.

Title ┈┈┈┈

My _____

: The title gives us the topic of the essay.

Topic Sentence ┈┈┈┈

Today _____ .

: The topic sentence gives us the main idea of the essay.

Body ┈┈┈┈

The event:

What is it?	It is a _____ .	party / lesson
Who is there?	My _____ are there.	friends / mother
Doing what?	They are playing _____ .	music / games
What else?	They are _____ .	sleeping / talking
Food:	I want to eat my _____ .	pie / cake
What else?	I have to blow out the _____ .	candles / light
	I want to open my _____ .	door / presents

: The body of the essay gives us the details about the topic.

Closing Sentence ┈┈┈┈

My _____ !

: The closing sentence finishes the essay. It can be a statement or an opinion.

Grammar Point

be verbs

	singular	plural
first person	I <u>am</u>	we <u>are</u>
second person	you <u>are</u>	you <u>are</u>
third person	he/she/it <u>is</u>	they <u>are</u>

Tip◆ In present tense, a "be" verb changes to "am," "are," and "is." In past tense, a "be" verb changes to "was" and "were."

action verbs

read, jump, play, study, go, run ...

I <u>enjoy</u> reading books.
She <u>brushes</u> her teeth every morning.
They often <u>go</u> out for a walk.

Tip◆ These types of verbs are called "**action verbs**." In present progressive tense, they can be in the "~ing" form. If the subject is third-person singular, "-s" or "-es" is added to the end of the verbs.

 Write the following verbs in the correct box.

Word Box	cry	speak	am	jump	is	are
	throw	was	sleep	talk	were	smile

Action verbs

Be verbs

 Circle the action verb and underline the "be" verb in each sentence.

Example Jamie <u>is</u> a carpenter. He (works) with wood.

1 She is a doctor. She helps sick people.

2 I am a dancer. I dance on the stage.

3 He is a singer. He sings beautifully.

4 We are college students. We study math.

5 You are French. You speak French.

Building Sentences 1

 A Look at the pictures and complete the sentences using the phrases in the box.

> **Word Box**   win first prize   buy a new computer   go to sleep   eat something delicious

1

I'm sleepy.

↘ I want to _____ .

2

I'm hungry.

↘ I _____ .

3

I always lose.

↘ I _____ .

4

My computer often breaks down.

↘ I _____ .

 B Look at the pictures and complete the sentences using the phrases in the box.

> **Word Box**   **A** the gym   **B** the movie theater   **C** the library
> do some exercise   watch a movie   read books

1

We are _____ . (place)

We are _____ . (action)

2

We are _____ . (place)

We are _____ . (action)

3

We are _____ . (place)

We are _____ . (action)

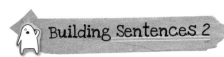

 A Match the phrases and write the sentences.

1 I am on •	• very interesting.
2 My teacher •	• look at the paintings.
3 We are visiting •	• a school trip.
4 I want to •	• is here.
5 The museum is •	• a museum.

1 _____

2 _____

3 _____

4 _____

5 _____

 B Complete the sentences using the phrases in the box.

at Jamsil Sports Complex	eat some popcorn
is very exciting	I have to wait for the break time
are here	cheering, singing, and shouting
trip to the basketball game	

My   trip to the basketball game

Today, I am _____ .

My friends _____ .

We are _____ .

I want to _____ .

But first, _____ .

The game _____ !

Writing

A Describe an event.

1 What event will you describe? _____

(e.g. a sports match, a birthday party, a school trip)

2 Why is today special? _____

(e.g. birthday, Saturday, school vacation)

3 Where are you? _____

(e.g. classroom, movie theater, school gym)

4 Who is with you? _____

(e.g. friends, family, teacher)

5 What are you doing? _____

(e.g. visiting a museum, playing music, watching a movie)

6 What verbs describe everybody?

ⓐ _____

ⓑ _____

ⓒ _____

(e.g. shout, run, sit, read)

7 What do you want to do?

_____

(e.g. look at the paintings, score a goal, eat some food)

8 What do you have to do first?

_____

(e.g. get the ball and run fast, wash your hands, sit at the table)

9 What else do you want to do?

_____

(e.g. have a rest, see my friend, have a drink)

10 How is the event? _____

(e.g. exciting, boring, interesting, scary, fun)

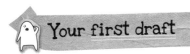

A Use your brainstorming to complete your draft. Look at the sample text and write your sentences in the same way.

Sample Text	Your Draft
Title	**Title**
My Birthday Party	1. _____
Topic Sentence	**Topic Sentence**
Today is my birthday.	2. _____
Body	**Body**
I am at my birthday party.	3. _____
My friends are here.	4. _____
We are playing games.	5. _____
We are all laughing, talking, and singing.	6. _____
My mom made a delicious birthday cake. I want to eat it now.	7. _____
But first, I have to blow out the candles and make a wish.	8. _____
I also want to open my presents!	9. _____
Closing Sentence	**Closing Sentence**
My birthday party is fun!	10. _____

Editing tips
* Remember that "action" verbs can be in the "~ing" form.

National English Ability Test

Look at pictures 1 and **2**, and describe what you see. Then imagine and write what will happen next.

Word Count

Unit

05

A New MP3 Player

I have a new MP3 player. My father bought it for me. I think it is expensive! The MP3 player is white, and it is very shiny. It is a small MP3 player, and it is not heavy. It has a square display screen. It also has four buttons. It is a very beautiful MP3 player! I like it because I can listen to music all the time.

A New MP3 Player

Warm-up

 Picture Description

A Look at the picture carefully and choose the correct words.

1 The MP3 player is linked to _____ . | headsets / earphones |

2 The MP3 player is _____ . | shiny / dark |

3 The MP3 player is _____ . | round / square |

4 The MP3 player is for _____ music. | listening to / singing |

B Look at the picture and complete the sentences using the words in the box.

Word Box	big	four	light	white

1 My old MP3 player was heavy, but my new one is _____ .

2 My old MP3 player was small, but my new one is _____ .

3 My old MP3 player was black, but my new one is _____ .

4 My old MP3 player had three buttons, but my new one has _____ .

Building Vocabulary

A Match each word to the correct picture.

1 **square** _____

2 **diamond** _____

3 **pentagon** _____

4 **triangle** _____

5 **round** _____

6 **oval** _____

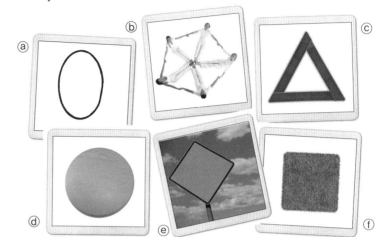

B Look at the pictures and fill in the blanks using the words in the box.

| Word Box | dirty / clean | high / low | heavy / light | huge / tiny |

1

3

2

4

Read the Text

A New MP3 Player   Title

I have a new MP3 player.   Topic Sentence

My father bought it for me.

I think it was expensive!

The MP3 player is white, and it is very shiny.

It is a small MP3 player, and it is not heavy.

It has a square display screen. It also has four buttons.

Body

It is a very beautiful MP3 player!

I like it because I can listen to music all the time.

Closing Sentence

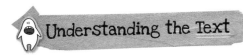

 A Answer the questions like the example.

> **Example**   Who bought the new MP3 player for you?
>
> ↘ _____My father_____ bought the new MP3 player for me.

1 Do you think it is cheap or expensive?

↘ I think _____ .

2 What is the color of the new MP3 player?

↘ It _____ .

3 What is the shape of the display screen?

↘ It _____ .

4 How many buttons does the new MP3 player have?

↘ It _____ .

5 Why do you like the new MP3 player?

↘ I like it _____ !

B Are these statements TRUE or FALSE?

1 The new MP3 player cost a lot of money.   True ☐   False ☐

2 It has a shiny surface.   True ☐   False ☐

3 It has many buttons, and it is heavy.   True ☐   False ☐

4 It is a beautiful MP3 player, but I don't like it very much. True ☐   False ☐

5 Only sometimes I can listen to music with the MP3 player.   True ☐   False ☐

Complete the Outline

 Fill in the blanks to complete the outline.

Title ----- A New _____

: The title gives us the topic of the essay.

Topic Sentence ----- I have _____ .

: The topic sentence tells us what the essay is about.

Body -----

Item:	_____	MP3 player / cellular phone
From whom:	_____	my father / my grandfather
Cost:	_____	cheap / expensive
Color:	_____	white / black
Size:	_____	huge / small
Weight:	_____	heavy / not heavy
Shape of the display screen:	_____	round / square
General appearance:	_____	beautiful / ugly

: The body of the essay gives us the details about the topic.

Closing Sentence ----- I like it because _____ .

: The closing sentence finishes the essay. It can be a statement or an opinion.

Grammar Point

Adjectives are words that describe or give us information about a noun or pronoun. Often, they give us information about size/shape, state/appearance, amount/number, quality, or color.

size / shape	big, small, huge, tiny, square...
state / appearance	new, old, shiny, dark, loud, quiet, happy, sad...
amount / number	much, many, little, a little, few, a few, one, two, three...
quality	excellent, good, bad, average...
color	red, brown, yellow, black, white...

Tip◆ Most commonly, an adjective comes before the noun.   e.g.) a cute baby

A Look at the pictures and choose the correct adjectives in the boxes.

1

It is a _____ face.   red / black

2

It is a _____ dog.   wet / dry

3

He is a _____ boy.   ugly / handsome

4

She is a _____ woman.   happy / sad

B Rewrite the sentences using the given adjectives.

1 It's a ship. (big)   ↘ It's _____ .

2 He is a student. (good)   ↘ He is _____ .

3 Julie is a nurse. (very, kind) ↘ Julie is _____ .

4 This is a car. (his nice)   ↘ This is _____ .

5 BoA is a singer. (very, famous) ↘ BoA is _____ .

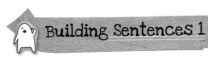

A Look at the pictures and complete the sentences using the words in the box.

Word Box	square	white	blue	round
	rectangular	black	triangular	pink

1

The MP3 player is _____, and it has a _____ display screen.

2

The MP3 player is _____, and it has a _____ display screen.

3

The MP3 player is _____, and it has a _____ display screen.

4

The MP3 player is _____, and it has a _____ display screen.

 Match the phrases and write the sentences.

1 I can surf the Internet ●		ⓐ using my new MP3 player.
2 I can listen to the songs ●		ⓑ using my new laptop.
3 I can look up the words ●		ⓒ using my USB stick.
4 I can save a lot of data ●		ⓓ using my electronic dictionary.

1 _____

2 _____

3 _____

4 _____

Building Sentences 2

A Look at the picture and fill in the blanks using the words in the box.

| Word Box | big | pictures | black | strap | bought | camera |

My mom _____ a new digital

_____ for me as a birthday present.

The digital camera is _____, and it

has a _____ lens. It also has a very

long _____. I like it because I can take

_____ of my family.

B Rewrite the sentences using the antonyms of the underlined adjectives.

(antonym: a word that means the opposite of another word)

1 My father bought an <u>old</u> MP3 player for me yesterday.

↳ _____

2 My new MP3 player is <u>cheap</u>.

↳ _____

3 It is shiny, and it has a <u>small</u> screen.

↳ _____

4 It is <u>white</u>, and it has four buttons.

↳ _____

5 It is a very <u>ugly</u> MP3 player.

↳ _____

Writing

A Describe an item.

1 What item will you describe? _____

(e.g. a bag, a TV, a desk, a new shirt)

2 Who bought it? _____

(e.g. parents, I, brother)

3 Do you think it is cheap or expensive?

_____

4 What color is it? _____

5 How does it look? _____

(e.g. dull, shiny, ugly)

6 Is it heavy or light? _____

7 What size or shape is it? _____

(e.g. big, thin, round, square)

8 What does it have? (adjective / noun)

1) _____

2) _____

(e.g. blue handle / long strap, square screen / six buttons)

9 It is: Choose one ✓

☐ beautiful

☐ ugly

☐ wonderful

☐ gorgeous

☐ _____ (your word)

10 Why do you like it? _____

(e.g. easy to use, very useful, good for me)

Use your brainstorming to complete your draft. Look at the sample text and write your sentences in the same way.

Sample Text	Your Draft

Title

A New MP3 Player

Topic Sentence

I have a new MP3 player.

Body

My father bought it for me.

I think it was expensive!

The MP3 player is white, and it is very shiny.

It is a small MP3 player, and it is not heavy.

It has a square display screen.

It also has four buttons.

It is a very beautiful MP3 player!

Closing Sentence

I like it because I can listen to music all the time.

Title

_____

Topic Sentence

1. _____

Body

2. _____

3. _____

4, 5. _____
_____

6, 7. _____
_____

8. _____

9. _____

Closing Sentence

10. _____

Editing tips

- Adjectives give us information about size/shape, state/appearance, amount/number, quality, color and so on.
- Remember that an adjective most commonly comes before the noun.

65

National English Ability Test

Your teacher has asked you to do some volunteer work. Choose one of the illustrations and write your response using the given words. Your response should be about 20 words and include two or three sentences.

①    ②    ③

clean the street	help	do paperwork
difficult	nursing home	the public office

Word Count

Unit 06

My Favorite Hobby

In my free time, I love to go fishing. It is very relaxing. I go fishing every weekend with Steve and Tony. We go to Lake Park. There are two lakes at Lake Park. There are lots of fish in the lake. We use two fishing rods and a fishing net. I always take a lunch box. Steve and Tony take their lunch boxes, too! Fishing is my favorite hobby.

Warm-up

 picture Description

A Look at the picture carefully and answer the questions.

| Example | Are the children skiing or fishing? ⤷ The children are ___fishing___ . |

1 How many children are there?

⤷ There are _____.

2 How many fishing rods are there?

⤷ There are _____.

3 How many fish do they have in the fishing net?

⤷ They have _____.

B Look at the picture carefully. Are these statements TRUE or FALSE?

1 One boy is looking at his watch. True ☐ False ☐

2 The children have blue fishing rods. True ☐ False ☐

3 The boys are fishing with two fishing rods and a fishing net. True ☐ False ☐

Building Vocabulary

 A Match each word to the correct picture.

1 hook _____

2 net _____

3 fishing rod _____

4 lake _____

5 earthworm _____

6 basket _____

 B Look at the pictures and fill in the blanks using plurals.

1

a child _____

2

a watch _____

3

a cup _____

4

a fish _____

Reading and Understanding

 Read the **T**ext

 My Favorite Hobby   Title

In my free time, I love to go fishing.   Topic Sentence

It is very relaxing. I go fishing every weekend with Steve and Tony. We go to Lake Park. There are two lakes at Lake Park. There are lots of fish in the lake. We use two fishing rods and a fishing net. I always take a lunch box. Steve and Tony take their lunch boxes, too!

Fishing is my favorite hobby.   Closing Sentence

Journal Contents

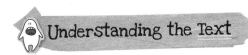
Understanding the Text

A Choose the correct words in the boxes and complete the sentences.

Example   I   go fishing   in my free time.   go fishing / go horse riding / go swimming

1   I go fishing _____ .   every day / every weekend / on Sunday

2   Fishing is _____ .   very boring / very exciting / very relaxing

3   I go fishing with my _____ .   two friends / two brothers / two sons

4   There are _____ at the park.   two rivers / two lakes / two ponds

5   We use _____ fishing rods.   one / two / three

6   I _____ .   take a lunch box / eat lunch at the restaurant

B Are these statements TRUE or FALSE?

1   Fishing is my favorite hobby.   True ☐   False ☐

2   We go to Lake Park for taking a walk.   True ☐   False ☐

3   There are not many fish in the lake.   True ☐   False ☐

4   I always take a lunch box when I go fishing.   True ☐   False ☐

5   Tony usually doesn't take his lunch box.   True ☐   False ☐

Complete the Outline

 Fill in the blanks to complete the outline.

Title ------ My _____

: The title gives us the topic of the journal.

Topic Sentence ------ In my free time _____.

: The topic sentence gives us the main idea of the text.

Body ------

Going fishing:

It is _____.   exciting / relaxing

How often: every _____   weekend / weekday

With whom: with my _____   brothers / friends

Details:

• _____ lakes at Lake Park   two / three

• _____ fish   not many / lots of

• using two _____   nets / fishing rods

• taking a _____   hamburger / lunch box

: The body of the journal gives us the details about the topic.

Closing Sentence ------ _____ is my favorite hobby.

: The closing sentence finishes the journal. It can be a statement or an opinion.

Grammar Point

* **Plurals** are used to show that there is more than one of something.

Most plurals are made by adding an **'s.'**:

    one cup ⇨ two cup**s**   one house ⇨ two house**s**

If the word ends in **'x,' 'sh,' 'ch'** or **'s,'** add **'es.'**:

    one fox ⇨ two fox**es**   one di**sh** ⇨ two di**shes**

    one wat**ch** ⇨ two wat**ches**   one bu**s** ⇨ two bu**ses**

If the word ends in a **consonant and then a 'y,'** delete the 'y' and add **'ies.'**:

    one la**dy** ⇨ two la**dies**   one pup**py** ⇨ two pup**pies**

    one hob**by** ⇨ two hob**bies**

There are some words that do not follow any of these rules. They are **'irregular.'**:

    one man ⇨ two **men**   one foot ⇨ two **feet**

    one mouse ⇨ two **mice**   one fish ⇨ two **fish**

A Write the plural form of each word.

1 one bowl   —   two _____   **2** one crayon   —   two _____

3 one man   —   two _____   **4** one box   —   two _____

5 one body   —   two _____   **6** one bush   —   two _____

7 one tooth   —   two _____   **8** one fish   —   two _____

B Look at the pictures and complete the sentences using given words.

1 There are _____ on the table. (book)

2 There are _____ in the room. (boy)

3 There is _____ by the door. (woman)

4 There are _____ in the cage. (mouse)

Building Sentences 1

A Look at the pictures and complete the sentences using the phrases in the box.

| Word Box | go hiking | ride a bicycle | go shopping | grow flowers |

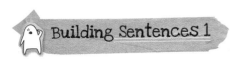

1 My grandfather _____ every day.

2 My sisters _____ every weekend.

3 I _____ once a month.

4 My brother _____ two days a week.

B Look at Jane's schedule and complete the sentences using the words in the box.

| Word Box | always | usually | often | sometimes | never |

Jane's schedule	SUN	MON	TUE	WED	THU	FRI	SAT
go jogging	✓	✓	✓	✓	✓	✓	✓
walk the dog	✓	✓		✓	✓		✓
go swimming	✓		✓		✓		✓
play tennis	✓			✓			
play computer games							

1 Jane _____ .

2 Jane _____ .

3 Jane _____ .

4 Jane _____ .

5 Jane _____ .

A Look at the pictures and complete the sentences using the phrases in the box.

Word Box	making model airplanes	painting	flying kites
	cooking	playing baseball	going camping

1 Josh likes _____ with his friends.

2 My friend and I enjoy _____ .

3 I love _____ very much.

4 Sam loves _____ .

5 They like _____ .

6 My kid enjoys _____ .

B Correct the mistakes and rewrite the sentences.

1 My grandfather likes collecting coin.

↘ _____

2 I have two hobbys: reading bookes and writing.

↘ _____

3 My brother raises two dog, five fish, and three hamsteres.

↘ _____

Writing

A Write about your hobby.

1 What is your favorite hobby? _____

(e.g. playing[to play] music, watch[to watch] movies)

2 Describe your hobby. _____

(e.g. exciting, interesting, relaxing, fun)

3 How often do you do your hobby?

_____

(e.g. every day, on Sundays, every other evening)

4 Who does your hobby with you?

_____

(e.g. parents, friends, David, by myself)

5 Where are you when you do your hobby?

_____

(e.g. at home, on a mountain, at the community center)

6 What are there?

1) _____

2) _____

(e.g. a park, lots of trees, buildings, people)

7 Do you use anything for your hobby?

Yes ☐ (go to question 8)

No ☐ (go to question 9)

8 What is it? _____

(e.g. a piano, walking boots, a camera, a racket)

9 What do you always do? _____

(e.g. eat snacks, laugh with my friends, go home late)

A Use your brainstorming to complete your draft. Look at the sample text and write your sentences in the same way.

Sample Text	Your Draft
Title	**Title**
My Favorite Hobby	
Topic Sentence	**Topic Sentence**
In my free time, I love to go fishing.	1.
Body	**Body**
It is very relaxing.	2.
I go fishing every weekend with Steve and Tony.	3, 4.
We go to Lake Park.	5.
There are two lakes at Lake Park.	6.
There are lots of fish in the lake.	
We use two fishing rods and a fishing net.	7, 8.
I always take a lunch box. Steve and Tony take their lunch boxes, too!	9.
Closing Sentence	**Closing Sentence**
Fishing is my favorite hobby.	

Editing tips
- Remember to follow the rules to form plurals.
- Remember to use indefinite articles "a, an" before a countable singular noun.

National English Ability Test

Look at the picture carefully and describe what the people are doing. (20~30 words)

There are some people at the concert hall.

A man with a black jacket _____(1)_____.

Two girls with long blonde hair _____(2)_____.

A tall woman _____(3)_____.

A boy with a yellow coat _____(4)_____.

Word Count

(1)

(2)

(3)

(4)

My Favorite Animals!

Dogs and lizards are my favorite pets. I have two dogs. They are friendly. They are also fluffy and clever. My dogs move their tails, so I know they are happy! I have a lizard, too. I like it because it is fast and quiet. Lizards never make noise. My cousin has cats, but I don't like them. They are cute, but they scare me. I love my pets, and they are my best friends.

Unit 07 I Like Dogs and ...

Warm-up

 Picture Description

A Look at the picture carefully and answer the questions.

1 How many cats and dogs are there?

↘ There are _____ cats and _____ dogs.

2 What color are the dogs?

↘ One is _____ and the other is _____ .

3 Which are bigger, the dogs or the cats?

↘ _____ are bigger.

B Look at the picture carefully. Are these statements TRUE or FALSE?

1 One dog has a long tail.　　　　　　　True ☐　　　False ☐

2 There are some yellow flowers.　　　　True ☐　　　False ☐

3 The girl is holding the dogs.　　　　　True ☐　　　False ☐

Building Vocabulary

 Match each word to the correct picture.

1 tail _____

2 beak _____

3 wing _____

4 fin _____

5 claw _____

6 feather _____

ⓐ ⓑ ⓒ ⓓ ⓔ ⓕ

 Match each picture to the correct word.

1 _____

ⓐ lizard

ⓒ hamster

4 _____

2 _____

ⓑ peacock

ⓕ puppy

5 _____

3 _____

ⓔ elephant

ⓓ dolphin

6 _____

Reading and Understanding

My Favorite Animals! **Title**

Dogs and lizards are my favorite pets. **Topic Sentence**

I have two dogs. They are friendly. They are also fluffy and clever. My dogs move their tails, so I know they are happy! I have a lizard, too. I like it because it is fast and quiet. Lizards never make noise. My cousin has cats, but I don't like them. They are cute, but they scare me.

Body

I love my pets, and they are my best friends. **Closing Sentence**

A Answer the questions like the example.

> **Example**   What animals do you like?
>
>   ↘ I like _____ dogs and lizards _____.

1 How many dogs do you have?

   ↘ I have _____.

2 Why do you like dogs?

   ↘ They are _____.

3 What do your dogs do when they are happy?

   ↘ They _____.

4 Why do you like lizards?

   ↘ They are _____.

5 Who has cats?

   ↘ _____ has cats.

B Are these statements TRUE or FALSE?

1 I raise dogs, a lizard, and cats as pets.   True ☐   False ☐

2 Lizards are quiet animals.   True ☐   False ☐

3 Lizards move very slowly.   True ☐   False ☐

4 I think dogs are smart animals.   True ☐   False ☐

5 Cats are cute, but I'm afraid of them.   True ☐   False ☐

6 My cousin has lizards, too.   True ☐   False ☐

Complete the Outline

 Fill in the blanks to complete the outline.

Title - - - - - My Favorite _____ !

: The title gives us the topic of the essay.

Topic Sentence - - - - - Dogs and lizards _____ .

: The topic sentence gives us the main idea of the essay.

Body - - - - -
How many dogs: _____

Character: (friendly, kind, cute, clever, lazy, noisy)

_____

Trait:

(excited - wagging its tail, sad - lying under the couch, stressed - biting its tail)

_____

What other pets: _____

Character: (friendly, kind, cute, clever, lazy, quiet, fast)

_____

My cousin's pet: _____

Character: (friendly, kind, cute, clever, lazy)

_____

: The body of the essay gives us the details about the topic.

Closing Sentence - - - - - I love my _____ .

: The closing sentence finishes the essay. It can be a statement or an opinion.

Grammar Point

• Conjunctions are "joining" words. They connect words, phrases, and clauses.

and: as well as
⇨ I like cats as well as dogs.
⇨ I like dogs **and** (I like) cats.

but: in contrast
⇨ I like yellow. In contrast, I don't like red.
⇨ I like yellow, **but** I don't like red.

because: for the reason that
⇨ I like math for the reason that it is fun.
⇨ I like math **because** it is fun.

so: and therefore
⇨ My friend did not come, and therefore I went alone.
⇨ My friend did not come **so** I went alone.

A Circle the conjunction in each sentence.

1 He is good at science, but he is not good at English.

2 I am hungry so I will eat a banana.

3 She does not like kimchi because it is spicy.

B Combine the sentences using the given conjunction.

| Example | I want to play outside. It is raining. | but |

↘ _____ I want to play outside, but it is raining _____ .

---

1 I am tired. I will go to bed soon. | so |

↘ _____

2 He cannot come. He is working. | because |

↘ _____

3 I love mountains. I love rivers. | and |

↘ _____

4 I like music. I don't like sports. | but |

↘ _____

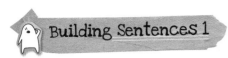

Building Sentences 1

 A Look at the pictures and complete the sentences like the example.

Example My favorite animal is a goldfish.

1 _____

2 _____

3 _____

4 _____

5 _____

 B Complete the sentences using the words in the box.

| **Word Box** | quiet | cute | clever | scary | fast |

1 I like cheetahs. They are not slow. They are _____.

2 I like turtles. They are not noisy. They are _____.

3 I don't like sharks. They are not safe. They are _____.

4 I like koalas. They are not ugly. They are _____.

5 I like dolphins. They are not stupid. They are _____.

Building Sentences 2

A Look at the pictures and match the phrases to make correct sentences.

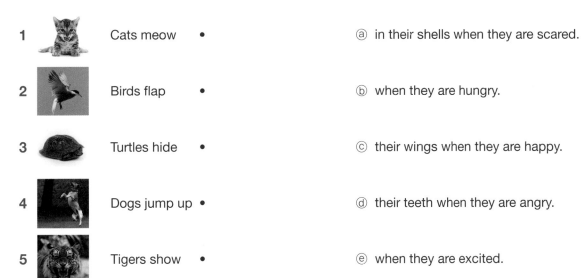

1   Cats meow •

2   Birds flap •

3   Turtles hide •

4   Dogs jump up •

5   Tigers show •

ⓐ in their shells when they are scared.

ⓑ when they are hungry.

ⓒ their wings when they are happy.

ⓓ their teeth when they are angry.

ⓔ when they are excited.

B Use the words in the boxes to complete the sentences. The words in the boxes may not be in the correct order.

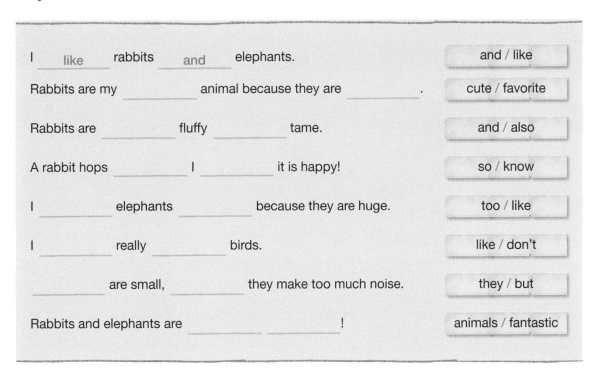

I ___like___ rabbits ___and___ elephants.

Rabbits are my _____ animal because they are _____ .

Rabbits are _____ fluffy _____ tame.

A rabbit hops _____ I _____ it is happy!

I _____ elephants _____ because they are huge.

I _____ really _____ birds.

_____ are small, _____ they make too much noise.

Rabbits and elephants are _____ !

and / like

cute / favorite

and / also

so / know

too / like

like / don't

they / but

animals / fantastic

Writing

 Brainstorming ‹Pair Work›

A Write about your favorite animal.

1 Which TWO animals do you like?

_____ and _____

(e.g. hamsters, cats, lions, giraffes, polar bears)

2 Do you raise your favorite animal?

Yes ☐ (go to question 3)   No ☐ (go to question 4)

3 How many of each animal do you have?

_____

4 Which one is your favorite animal? _____

5 What TWO words describe your favorite animal?

_____ and _____

(e.g. clever, happy, fun, graceful, beautiful, fast, slow, quiet)

6 How do you know when this animal is happy?

_____

(e.g. wags its tail, plays nicely, cleans its paws, bark aloud)

7 Why do you like the other animal? _____

(e.g. strong, clever, pretty, cute, beautiful)

8 Which animal don't you like? _____

(e.g. snakes, pigeons, mice, lizards, crocodiles)

9 What is a good thing about the animal you don't like?

_____

(e.g. cute, clever, strong, quiet, smart, swift, fluffy)

10 What is a bad thing about this animal? _____

(e.g. lazy, smelly, scary, noisy, dirty)

11 Which word best describes your favorite animal?

_____

(e.g. wonderful, exciting, playful, lovely, beautiful)

A Use your brainstorming to complete your draft. Look at the sample text and write your sentences in the same way.

Sample Text	Your Draft
Title	**Title**
My Favorite Pets	
Topic Sentence	**Topic Sentence**
Dogs and lizards are my favorite pets.	1.
Body	**Body**
I have two dogs. They are friendly. They are also fluffy and clever.	2, 3, 4, 5
My dogs move their tails, so I know they are happy!	6.
I have a lizard, too. I like it because it is fast and quiet. Lizards never make noise.	3, 7.
My cousin has cats, but I don't like them. They are cute, but they scare me.	8. 9, 10.
Closing Sentence	**Closing Sentence**
I love my pets, and they are my best friends.	11.

Editing tips

- Remember to use the correct "joining words" called conjunctions.
- Use proper adjectives to describe your pets.

National English Ability Test

You are going to have a birthday party next week. Write an invitation letter to your friends. (about 30 words)

Dear friend,

_____

_____

_____

_____

_____

Word Count

Unit
O8

Getting a Report Card

This is how my friends and I feel today. I feel wonderful today because I have the highest score on the test. I always study very hard. But John feels sad because he has a bad grade. He plays too many computer games, so he doesn't study enough. Sandy feels nervous because her parents are strict. She has a good grade, but she hasn't scored 100%. Leo feels excited because he has a better score than John! We all feel different because of our test scores.

Warm-up

 Picture Description

A Look at the picture and match the phrases to make correct sentences.

1 One boy is   •   ⓐ happy.

2 The other   •   ⓑ is nervous.

3 One girl   •   ⓒ boy is sad.

4 The other   •   ⓓ girl is excited.

B Look at the picture carefully. Are these statements TRUE or FALSE?

1 Two boys have black hair.   True ☐   False ☐

2 Four students are holding report cards.   True ☐   False ☐

3 One boy and one girl are crying.   True ☐   False ☐

Building Vocabulary

A Match each word to the correct picture.

1 **question mark** _____

2 **taking a test** _____

3 **cheating** _____

4 **answer sheet** _____

5 **bad grade** _____

6 **studying hard** _____

 Look at the pictures and fill in the blanks using the words in the box.

| Word Box | **A** excited | bored | disappointed |

1

He looks _____.

2

She is _____.

3

He seems _____.

| Word Box | **B** angry | lonely | nervous |

4

He looks _____.

5

She is _____.

6

She feels _____.

Reading and Understanding

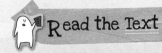 **R**ead the **T**ext

Getting a Report Card   Title

This is how my friends and I feel today.   Topic Sentence

I feel wonderful today because I have the highest score on the test.

I always study very hard.

But John feels sad because he has a bad grade. He plays too many

computer games, so he doesn't study enough.

Sandy feels nervous because her parents are strict. She has a good

grade, but she hasn't scored 100%.

Leo feels excited because he has a better score than John!

We all feel different because of our test scores.   Closing Sentence

 Body

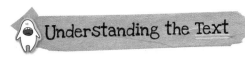

A Answer the questions like the example.

Example   Why do you feel wonderful today?

↘ I feel wonderful because ___I have the highest score on the test___ .

1 Why does John feel sad?

↘ He feels sad because _____ .

2 Why does John have a bad grade?

↘ He has a bad grade because _____ .

3 Why does Sandy feel nervous?

↘ She feels nervous because _____ .

4 Why does Leo feel excited?

↘ He feels excited because _____ .

5 What makes them feel different?

↘ _____

B Are these statements TRUE or FALSE?

1 I never study very hard, but I usually get a good grade.   True ☐   False ☐

2 John did not do well on the test.   True ☐   False ☐

3 Getting a bad grade makes John feel sad.   True ☐   False ☐

4 Sandy scored 100% on the test.   True ☐   False ☐

5 John has a worse score than Leo.   True ☐   False ☐

6 Everybody feels the same today.   True ☐   False ☐

Complete the Outline

 Fill in the blanks to complete the outline.

Title ---- Getting a Report Card

: The title gives us the topic of the essay.

Topic Sentence ---- This is _____ .

: The topic sentence tells us what the essay is about.

Body

My feeling: _____

Why? _____

What you do: _____

John's feeling: _____

Why? _____

What he does: _____

Sandy's feeling: _____

Why? _____

Leo's feeling: _____

Why? _____

: The body of the essay gives us the details about the topic.

Closing Sentence ---- _____

: The closing sentence finishes the essay. It can be a statement or an opinion.

Grammar Point

Simple present tense is used to describe things that happen repeatedly, or are long-lasting, or are about people and things in general.

subject	verb	example
I, you, we, they	walk	I walk to school. They walk to school.
he, she, it	play+s	He plays basketball. She plays the drums.

Tip◆ When the subject is the third person singular like he, she, it, Mary, John, Leo etc., verbs that end in 's,' 'sh,' 'ch,' 'x,' or 'z' have '+es.' e.g. He watches soccer. It mixes soup. She passes the shops.

Tip◆ The verbs 'be,' 'do,' and 'have' are irregular. :
- be: I am, you are, we are, they are, he/she/it is
- do: I do, you do, we do, they do, he/she/it does
- have: I have, you have, we have, they have, he/she/it has

 Choose the correct verb.

1 This is how my friends and I (feel / feels) today.

2 I (am / is / are) happy because it (am / is / are) snowing.

3 He (do / does) his homework.

4 All of my friends (has / have) the same feelings today.

5 There (is / are) a lot of water in the pool.

 Complete the sentences using given verbs. (use present tense)

1 It _____ (do) not work.

2 I _____ (feel) very happy today.

3 You _____ (be) very kind.

4 She _____ (watch) movies every day.

5 They _____ (have) lots of clothes.

6 We _____ (dance) at the club.

7 He _____ (laugh at) funny things.

8 Mary _____ (look) nervous.

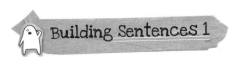

A Look at the pictures and complete the sentences using the words in the box.

Word Box	anxious	shocked	interested	lonely

1   She feels _____. She has no friends.

2   He feels _____ in books. He likes reading books.

3   She feels _____. She has a big test tomorrow.

4   He feels _____ because it's very big news.

B Look at the chart and fill in the blanks using the words in the box.

Word Box	better	highest	good	worse	worst

Math Test Results

Angela	Jacob	Clare	Kevin	Erica
95	82	75	68	87

1   Angela has the _____ score in the Math test.

2   Jacob has a _____ score than Kevin.

3   Clare has a _____ score than Jacob.

4   Kevin has the _____ score in the Math test.

5   Erica has a _____ score in the Math test.

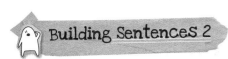 **Building Sentences 2**

 Look at the example and complete the sentences using the phrases in the box.

Word Box
is bored / her MP3 player is broken   *is happy / he got an allowance*
is angry / he lost his wallet   am hungry / I skipped lunch this afternoon
are tired / it was a long journey   is worrying / are late

Example   My brother ___is happy___ because ___he got an allowance___ .

1 My dad _____ because _____ .

2 My mom _____ because we _____ .

3 I _____ because _____ .

4 My grandparents _____ because _____ .

5 My sister _____ because _____ .

B Combine two sentences using "because."

Example   John is upset. John lost his book.

↘ John is upset ___because he lost his book___ .

1 Jason is exhausted. Jason walked to school.

↘ Jason is exhausted _____ .

2 Sally is disappointed. Sally didn't receive good grades.

↘ Sally is disappointed _____ .

3 Miss Green is nervous. Miss Green is having an interview.

↘ Miss Green is nervous _____ .

4 Harry and Becky are annoyed. Harry and Becky cannot turn on the computer.

↘ Harry and Becky are annoyed _____ .

Writing

Brainstorming ‹Pair Work›

A Describe feelings

1 Which group of people will you describe the feelings of?

_____ (e.g. friends, family, teachers)

2 How do you feel today?

_____

(e.g. sad, excited, upset)

3 Why do you feel like this?

_____

(e.g. lost my phone, went shopping, went to a concert, went on a picnic)

4 What do you always do?

_____

(e.g. forget things, buy my ticket online, study very hard)

5 Write the names of the people you are going to describe:

* Describe how they feel. Use the 'EMOTIONS' HELP BOX for ideas or choose your own.

* Why do they feel like this? Use the 'REASONS' HELP BOX for ideas or choose your own.

	NAME	EMOTIONS	REASONS
Ⓐ			
Ⓑ			
Ⓒ			
Ⓓ			

HELP BOX : EMOTIONS			**HELP BOX: REASONS**
happy	sad	nervous	playing computer games
calm	good	sleepy	going to a party
excited	bored	hopeful	finished his/her homework
shocked	annoyed	worried	visiting his/her family
			likes swimming
			has an exam

Your first draft

A Use your brainstorming to complete your draft. Look at the sample text and write your sentences in the same way.

Sample Text	Your Draft
Title	**Title**
Getting a Report Card	
Topic Sentence	**Topic Sentence**
This is how my friends and I feel today.	1.
Body	**Body**
I feel wonderful today because I have the highest score on the test.	2, 3.
I always study very hard.	
But John feels sad because he has a bad grade. He plays too many computer games, so he doesn't study enough.	4.
Sandy feels nervous because her parents are strict. She has a good grade, but she hasn't scored 100%.	5.
Leo feels excited because he has a better score than John!	
Closing Sentence	**Closing Sentence**
We all feel different because of our test scores.	

Editing tips

* Remember that the <u>emotion</u> must match the reason. You do not feel <u>happy</u> if you lose your phone!
* Remember to use the correct form of the verb in the simple present tense.

National English Ability Test

Look at pictures 1 and 2, and describe what you see. Then imagine and write what will happen next.

① ② ③

Word Count

Unit 09

My Vacation in Paris

I went to Paris on vacation last month. Paris is the capital of France. I stayed in a lovely hotel. I ate a lot of delicious food. I really liked the bread! I also saw the Eiffel Tower and a lot of beautiful old buildings. I visited a museum, too. At the museum I looked at a painting called the *Mona Lisa*. I had a wonderful vacation in Paris!

My Vacation in Paris

Warm-up

 Picture Description

A Look at the picture carefully and choose the correct words.

1 The Eiffel Tower is _____ .   tall / tiny / tool

2 There are lots of _____ .   fountains / buildings / towers

3 A woman is _____ the grass.   playing / lying on / sitting on

B Look at the picture carefully. Are these statements TRUE or FALSE?

1 It is raining heavily.   True ☐   False ☐

2 A man is taking a photo of the Eiffel Tower.   True ☐   False ☐

3 There are some people in a pond.   True ☐   False ☐

Building Vocabulary

A Match each word to the correct picture.

1 baggage _____

2 fountain _____

3 passport _____

4 bellhop _____

5 statue _____

6 museum _____

B Look at the pictures and fill in the blanks using the words in the box.

| Word Box | beach | mountain | desert | jungle | waterfalls | cave |

1 _____

2 _____

3 _____

4 _____

5 _____

6 _____

105

Reading and Understanding

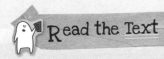 **R**ead the **T**ext

 My Vacation in Paris   Title

I went to Paris on vacation last month.   Topic Sentence

Paris is the capital of France. I stayed in a lovely hotel. I ate a lot

of delicious food. I really liked the bread!

I also saw the Eiffel Tower and a lot of beautiful old buildings.

I visited a museum, too. At the museum I looked at a painting

called the *Mona Lisa*.

I had a wonderful vacation in Paris!   Closing Sentence

Body

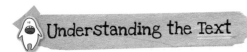

A Choose the correct words in the boxes and complete the sentences.

> **Example** When did you go on vacation?   last month / last year
>
> ↘ I went on vacation   last month   .

1 Where did you go on vacation?   Germany / France

↘ I went to _____ .

2 Where did you stay?   hotel / tent

↘ I stayed in a lovely _____ .

3 What did you like?   bread / noodles

↘ I liked the _____ .

4 What did you see?   rivers / buildings

↘ I saw a lot of beautiful old _____ .

5 Where did you visit?   museum / theater

↘ I visited a(n) _____ .

B Are these statements TRUE or FALSE?

1 I went to Paris to study French.   True ☐   False ☐

2 The capital of Italy is Paris.   True ☐   False ☐

3 I couldn't see many beautiful buildings.   True ☐   False ☐

4 I saw the painting, the *Mona Lisa* at the museum.   True ☐   False ☐

5 I went on my vacation with my sister.   True ☐   False ☐

Complete the Outline

 Fill in the blanks to complete the outline.

Title

My _____

: The title gives us the topic of the essay.

Topic Sentence

I went to _____ on vacation last month.

: The topic sentence gives us the main idea of the essay.

Body

About Paris: _____

Staying: _____

Eating: _____

Seeing: _____

Visiting: _____

: The body of the essay gives us the details about the topic.

Closing Sentence

I had a _____ !

: The closing sentence finishes the essay. It can be a statement or an opinion.

Grammar Point

Simple past tense is used to describe an event, action, or situation that happened in the past.

- **To make past tense verbs, simply add "-ed" with most verbs.**
  e.g. walk ⇨ walked   call ⇨ called

  However, you need to change the verb ending a little with some verbs.

verb ending	how to make the past tense	examples
e	add "-d"	arri**ved**, li**ved**, li**ked**...
consonant+y	change "y" to "i", then add "-ed"	stud**ied**, tr**ied**, cr**ied**...
one vowel+one consonant	double the consonant, then add "-ed"	stop**ped**, beg**ged**, plan**ned**...

- **Some verbs are irregular.**
  e.g. have ⇨ had   eat ⇨ ate   go ⇨ went   see ⇨ saw   sing ⇨ sang   do ⇨ did

 Circle all the past tense verbs in the text.

I went to Paris on vacation last month. Paris is the capital of France. I stayed in a lovely hotel. I ate a lot of delicious food. I really liked the bread! I also saw the Eiffel Tower and a lot of beautiful old buildings. I visited a museum, too. At the museum I looked at a painting called the *Mona Lisa*.

I had a wonderful vacation in Paris!

 Complete the sentences using past tense verbs.

Example	I go to school. ↘ I	went	to school.

1 I really want that pizza. ↘ I really _____ .

2 We wait for two hours. ↘ We _____ .

3 The girl sings beautifully. ↘ The girl _____ .

4 The boy has a red ball. ↘ The boy _____ .

5 He finishes his homework. ↘ He _____ .

6 My mother does the dishes. ↘ My mother _____ .

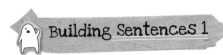

Building Sentences 1

 A Look at the example and complete the sentences using the words in the box.

| Word Box | China | *South Korea* | Australia | India | the U.S.A. |

Example   Seoul is _____ the capital of South Korea _____ .

1 Washington, D.C. is _____ .

2 Beijing is _____ .

3 New Delhi is _____ .

4 Canberra is _____ .

 B Look at the pictures and complete the sentences using the words in the box.
(Use past tense)

| Word Box | have a big lunch | rain heavily | cry a lot | watch TV too much | play baseball |

1   I _____ with my friends after school.

2   He _____ last weekend.

3   It _____ yesterday.

4   He _____ .

5   I _____ when I was young.

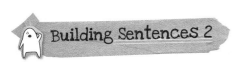

Building Sentences 2

A Put the words in the correct order to make correct sentences.

Example   My / Australia / in / vacation

    ↳ _____ My vacation in Australia _____

1   vacation / I / went / Australia / to / on / year / last

    ↳ _____

2   stayed / I / my / at / aunt's / house

    ↳ _____

3   really / in / playing / the garden / liked / I

    ↳ _____

4   Sydney Harbour / I / visited

    ↳ _____

5   had / fantastic / a / I / in / vacation / Australia

    ↳ _____

B Choose the correct words in the boxes and complete the sentences. (Use past tense.)

I ____went____ to ____Jejudo____ on vacation.	go / Jejudo
I _____ at my _____ house.	stay / friend's
I really _____ the _____ weather!	like / warm
I _____ a _____ and the sea.	see / waterfall
I also _____ a toy _____.	museum / visit
I _____ toys made from _____.	look at / paper
I _____ a _____ vacation in Jejudo.	have / great

111

Writing

 Brainstorming ‹Pair Work›

A Write about your vacation.

1 Where did you go on vacation? _____

(e.g. Beijing, Hawaii, Tokyo, Jejudo, Guam)

2 When did you go? _____

(e.g. last year, last month, two years ago)

3 What is this place? _____

(e.g. the capital of ..., an island, rural area, small town)

4 Where did you stay? _____

(e.g. in a hotel, at a friend's house, at an inn, at uncle's house)

5 What did you do? _____

(e.g. played games, ate food, swam in the sea, visited museums)

6 What did you really like? _____

(e.g. eating burgers, looking at ...)

7 What else did you do?

_____ and _____

(e.g. walked along the river, went snowboarding)

8 Where did you visit? _____

(e.g. the park, a lot of shops, a museum)

9 What did you do at this place? _____

(e.g. had a rest, looked at the view)

10 Choose the best description of your vacation.

_____

(e.g. enjoyable, interesting, relaxing, refreshing, unforgettable)

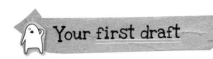 **Your first draft**

 A Use your brainstorming to complete your draft. Look at the sample text and write your sentences in the same way.

Sample Text	Your Draft
Title	**Title**
My Vacation in Paris	
Topic Sentence	**Topic Sentence**
I went to Paris on vacation last month.	1, 2.
Body	**Body**
Paris is the capital of France.	3.
I stayed in a lovely hotel.	4.
I ate a lot of delicious food.	5.
I really liked the bread!	6.
I also saw the Eiffel Tower and a lot of beautiful old buildings.	7.
I visited a museum, too.	8.
At the museum, I looked at a painting called the *Mona Lisa*.	9.
Closing Sentence	**Closing Sentence**
I had a wonderful vacation in Paris!	10.

Editing tips
- Remember that most past tense verbs are formed by: verb + "ed."
- Remember that some past tense verbs are irregular.

National English Ability Test

Today you have club activities after class. Choose one of the illustrations and write your response using the given words. Your response should be about 20 words and include two or three sentences.

①
②
③

watch a movie
at the theater

read a book
in the library

Taekwondo
at the gym

Word Count

Unit 10

My Plan for the Baseball Game

I am going to play baseball on Sunday. Here is my plan to get ready. First, I'm going to go jogging every morning. Second, I'm going to practice throwing and catching a ball on Monday. Third, I'm going to practice hitting with Dad on Tuesday and Thursday. Fourth, I'm going to relax on Saturday because I need a rest before having a baseball game. Finally, I'll hit a home run on Sunday. Right now, I think I'll wash my dirty uniform. I think I'll win the game with this perfect plan.

My plan for the Baseball Game

Warm-up

 Picture Description

A Look at the picture carefully and complete the sentences.

1 What letter is on the baseball cap?   The letter '＿＿＿＿＿' is on the cap.

2 How many baseball bats are there?   There are ＿＿＿＿＿ baseball bats.

3 What color is the baseball cap next to the bag?   The baseball cap is ＿＿＿＿＿.

B Look at the picture carefully. Are these statements TRUE or FALSE?

1 The baseball shirt has stripes.   True ☐   False ☐

2 The boy in red shirt is catching a baseball.   True ☐   False ☐

3 There are two baseballs next to the bag.   True ☐   False ☐

A Match each word to the correct picture.

1 **dribble** _____

2 **kick** _____

3 **shoot** _____

4 **catch** _____

5 **hit** _____

6 **jog** _____

ⓐ ⓑ ⓒ ⓓ ⓔ ⓕ

B Look at the pictures and fill in the blanks using the words in the box.

| Word Box | volleyball | table tennis | wrestling | marathon | field hockey | basketball |

1 _____

2 _____

3 _____

4 _____

5 _____

6 _____

Read the Text

My Plan for the Baseball Game `Title`

I am going to play baseball on Sunday. `Topic Sentence`

Here is my plan to get ready.

First, I'm going to go jogging every morning. Second, I'm going to practice throwing and catching a ball on Monday. Third, I'm going to practice hitting with Dad on Tuesday and Thursday. Fourth, I'm going to relax on Saturday because I need a rest before having a baseball game. Finally, I'll hit a home run on Sunday.

Right now, I think I'll wash my dirty uniform.

`Body` I think I'll win the game with this perfect plan. `Closing Sentence`

Home run!

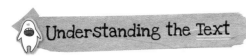

Understanding the Text

A Choose the words in the boxes and complete the sentences.

Example   What are you going to do every morning? | go jogging / practice hitting |

↘ I am going to _____ go jogging _____ .

---

1 What are you going to practice after school on Monday? | throwing and catching / hitting |

↘ I'm going to practice _____ a ball.

2 What are you going to practice on Tuesday and Thursday? | catching / hitting |

↘ I'm going to practice _____ .

3 Who is going to help you practice hitting? | Dad / My friend |

↘ _____ is going to help me practice hitting.

4 Why are you going to relax on Saturday? | practice / a rest |

↘ Because I need _____ before having a baseball game.

5 What will you do right now? | wash my uniform / go running |

↘ Right now, I think I will _____ .

B Are these statements TRUE or FALSE?

1 I am going to play baseball every morning.   True ☐   False ☐

2 I am going to practice throwing, catching, and hitting.   True ☐   False ☐

3 I need to wash my uniform.   True ☐   False ☐

4 I do not have time to relax.   True ☐   False ☐

5 I want to hit a home run on Sunday.   True ☐   False ☐

6 I think my plan is perfect.   True ☐   False ☐

Complete the Outline

 Fill in the blanks to complete the outline.

Title ----- My _____

: The title gives us the topic of the essay.

Topic Sentence ----- I am going to _____.

: The topic sentence gives us the main point of the essay.

Body

First: _____ every morning
> go jogging / go swimming

Second: practice _____
> throwing and catching / hitting

Third: practice _____ with Dad
> hitting / running

Fourth: _____ on Saturday
> exercising / relaxing

Finally: will _____
> hit a home run / score a goal

Right now: will _____
> wash my uniform / pack a bag

: The body gives us the details of what needs to be done.

Closing Sentence ----- I think I'll _____ with this perfect plan.

: The closing sentence finishes the essay.

Grammar Point

"Be going to" is used to say that someone has a **definite plan** to do something later on.

> I **am going to** study hard tonight.
>
> We **are going to** see the movie tomorrow at 7 pm.

Tip ◆ You must use the correct form of the verb 'be': 'I am,' 'we are' etc.

"Will" is used to say that someone **volunteers** to do something later on or decides to do something at the time of speaking/writing.

> I **will** help you with your homework.
>
> I **will** call you later.

 Complete the dialogs using either "be going to" or "will" and the given verbs.

1 A: I would like some coffee.

B: I _____ (get) it for you. (hint: volunteers)

2 A: What job do you want when you get older?

B: I _____ (be) a fashion model. (hint: definite plan)

3 A: We don't have any bread.

B: OK, I _____ (buy) some bread. (hint: volunteers)

4 A: What are we going to do tomorrow?

B: We _____ (visit) your grandparents. (hint: definite plan)

5 A: How can I get to the airport on Sunday? My car is broken.

B: Don't worry. I _____ (give) you a ride. (hint: volunteers)

6 A: When are you going to get married?

B: Ryan and I _____ (get married) in May. (hint: definite plan)

A Look at the pictures and complete the dialogs using "will" and the words in the box.

Word Box	snow	open	help	have

1

A: These boxes are heavy.

B: I _____ you.

2

A: Ready to order?

B: I _____ the strawberry flavor.

3

A: Look at the sky.

B: It _____ soon.

4

A: It's so hot in here.

B: I _____ the door for you.

B Look at Jenny's diary and complete the sentences using "be going to."

Jenny's diary

SUN	MON	TUE	WED	THU	FRI	SAT
visit my aunt	meet my English teacher	write a letter to Tom	study for the mid-term	take a test	go shopping with my sisters	borrow some books from the library

1 Jenny _____ on Sunday.

2 Jenny _____ on Monday.

3 Jenny _____ on Tuesday.

4 Jenny _____ on Wednesday.

5 Jenny _____ on Thursday.

6 Jenny _____ on Friday.

7 Jenny _____ on Saturday.

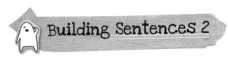

Building Sentences 2

 A Match the phrases and write the sentences.

1 Here is my plan •		ⓐ for today and tomorrow.
2 Today, I am •		ⓑ popcorn and Coke.
3 We are going •		ⓒ am going to church with Ben.
4 I will buy •		ⓓ going to visit my uncle.
5 Tomorrow, I •		ⓔ to watch a movie together.

1 _____

2 _____

3 _____

4 _____

5 _____

B Choose the phrases in the box and complete the essay.

Word Box	*am going to take*	am going to ask	am going to search
	will listen to	am going to set	am going to review
	am going to practice	am going to buy	am going to pack

I _____am going to take_____ an exam tomorrow.

Here is my plan to get ready.

First, I _____ the textbook.

Second, I _____ the Internet.

Third, I _____ my mom to help.

Fourth, I _____ some questions.

Fifth, I _____ some new pencils.

Sixth, I _____ my school bag.

Lastly, I _____ my alarm clock.

Right now, I think _____ music to relax.

Writing

 Brainstorming ‹Pair Work›

A Make a plan to do something.

1 What are you going to do? _____
   (e.g. go to Jeju Island, learn to play the guitar, make a kite)

2 When are you going to do it? _____
   (e.g. on Saturday, tomorrow, in March)

3 Choose the timescale for your plan.
   • first, second etc.   ☐
   • on Monday, on Tuesday etc.   ☐
   • in January, in February etc.   ☐
   • at 9 am, at 10 am etc.   ☐

4 What do you need to do to get ready?
   ⓐ _____
   ⓑ _____
   ⓒ _____
   ⓓ _____
                     (e.g. buy insurance, prepare first aid)

5 Finally, what are you going to do there?
   _____
                     (e.g. eat delicious food, visit an ancient tomb)

6 Right now, what will you do?
   _____
                     (e.g. pack my suitcase, write down my plan)

7 What do you think of your plan?
   _____
                     (e.g. perfect plan, enjoyable plan, great plan)

A Use your brainstorming to complete your draft. Look at the sample text and write your sentences in the same way.

Sample Text	Your Draft
Title	**Title**
My Plan for the Baseball Game	
Topic Sentence	**Topic Sentence**
I am going to play baseball on Sunday.	1, 2.
Body	**Body**
Here is my plan to get ready. First, I'm going to go jogging every morning. Second, I'm going to practice throwing and catching a ball on Monday. Third, I'm going to practice hitting with Dad on Tuesday and Thursday. Fourth, I'm going to relax on Saturday because I need a rest before having a baseball game. Finally, I'll hit a home run on Sunday. Right now, I think I'll wash my dirty uniform.	3, 4 ⓐ ⓑ ⓒ ⓓ 5 6
Closing Sentence	**Closing Sentence**
I think I'll win the game with this perfect plan.	7

Editing tips

- Remember to do the things in your plan in the correct order.
- Use "be going to" for definite plans and use "will" for something you decide at the time of speaking/writing.

Writing for NEAT

National English Ability Test

Look at the picture carefully and describe what the people are doing. (20~30 words)

A girl with a pink ribbon _____(1)_____.

A boy with glasses _____(2)_____.

Two students at the front _____(3)_____.

A boy by the window _____(4)_____.

Word Count

(1)

(2)

(3)

(4)

126

Memo!

Memo!

수준별 맞춤

Vocabulary 시리즈

The Voca
Level 1~7

This Is Vocabulary
초급, 중급, 고급, 어원편

Grammar 시리즈

Grammar 공감
Level 1~3

After School Grammar
Level 1~3

Grammar Bridge
Level 1~3

중학영문법 뽀개기
Level 1~3

The Grammar with Workbook
starter
Level 1~2

OK Grammar
Level 1~4

The Grammar
Starter
Level 1~3

This Is Grammar
초급 1·2
중급 1·2
고급 1·2

영작문 기초 **탄탄하게** 잡아주는

Smart
Writing

Workbook

전종삼 · 스티브 브라운 · 조금배 지음

1

NEXUS Edu

 Second Draft

Unit 1 My Best Friend

A Write Your Own.

B student's checklist

 Did you

- write a topic sentence? ☐
- use capital letters for proper nouns? ☐
- write a closing sentence? ☐
- check your spelling? ☐
- use punctuation correctly? ☐

Final Draft

Unit 1 My Best Friend

A Write Your Own.

B Teacher's checklist

Did the student:

- write clear and understandable English?
- use common and proper nouns correctly?
- write strong topic and closing sentences?
- describe his or her best friend adequately?
- spell all words correctly?

D Teacher's comments

C Teacher's mark

/ 5

 **Second Draft**

Unit 2 Making a Cake

 A Write Your Own.

 B student's checklist

Did you
- write a topic sentence?
- use capital letters for proper nouns?
- write a closing sentence?
- check your spelling?
- use punctuation correctly?

 **Final Draft**

Unit 2 Making a Cake

A Write Your Own.

 D Teacher's comments

 C Teacher's mark

/5

 **Second Draft**

Unit 3 My New Pen Pal

A Write Your Own.

B student's checklist

 Did you

- write a topic sentence? ☐
- use capital letters for proper nouns? ☐
- write a closing sentence? ☐
- check your spelling? ☐
- use punctuation correctly? ☐

 **Final Draft**

Unit 3 My New Pen Pal

A Write Your Own.

B Teacher's checklist

Did the student:

- write clear and understandable English?
- use personal pronouns correctly?
- write a correct greeting and sign-off?
- describe his or her family adequately?
- spell all words correctly?

 D Teacher's comments

 C Teacher's mark

/ 5

 **Second Draft**

Unit 4 My Birthday Party

 A Write Your Own.

 B student's checklist

Did you
- write a topic sentence? □
- use capital letters for proper nouns? □
- write a closing sentence? □
- check your spelling? □
- use punctuation correctly? □

Final Draft

Unit 4 My Birthday Party

A Write Your Own.

B Teacher's checklist

Did the student:
- write clear and understandable English?
- use "action verbs" and "be verbs" correctly?
- write strong topic and closing sentences?
- describe an event adequately?
- spell all words correctly?

D Teacher's comments

C Teacher's mark

/5

 Second Draft

Unit 5 A New MP3 Player

 Write Your Own.

 student's checklist

Did you

- write a topic sentence? ☐
- use capital letters for proper nouns? ☐
- write a closing sentence? ☐
- check your spelling? ☐
- use punctuation correctly? ☐

Final Draft

Unit 5 A New MP3 Player

A Write Your Own.

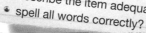

B Teacher's checklist

Did the student:

- write clear and understandable English?
- use relevant and appropriate adjectives?
- write strong topic and closing sentences?
- describe the item adequately?
- spell all words correctly?

D Teacher's comments

C Teacher's mark

/ 5

 **Second Draft**

Unit 6 In My Free Time

 Write Your Own.

 student's checklist

Did you

- write a topic sentence? ☐
- use capital letters for proper nouns? ☐
- write a closing sentence? ☐
- check your spelling? ☐
- use punctuation correctly? ☐

 **Final Draft**

Unit 6 In My Free Time

A Write Your Own.

 **Teacher's checklist**

Did the student:

- write clear and understandable English?
- form plurals correctly?
- write strong topic and closing sentences?
- describe his or her hobby adequately?
- spell all words correctly?

D Teacher's comments

 C Teacher's mark

/ 5

 **Second Draft**

Unit 7 I Like Dogs and ...

 Write Your Own.

 student's checklist

Did you
- write a topic sentence? ☐
- use capital letters for proper nouns? ☐
- write a closing sentence? ☐
- check your spelling? ☐
- use punctuation correctly? ☐

Final Draft

Unit 7 I Like Dogs and ...

A Write Your Own.

D Teacher's comments

C Teacher's mark

/ 5

A Write Your Own.

B student's checklist

 Did you

- write a topic sentence? ☐
- use capital letters for proper nouns? ☐
- write a closing sentence? ☐
- check your spelling? ☐
- use punctuation correctly? ☐

Final Draft

Unit 8 I feel ...

A Write Your Own.

B Teacher's checklist

Did the student:

- write clear and understandable English?
- use simple present tense correctly?
- write strong topic and closing sentences?
- describe feelings adequately?
- spell all words correctly?

D Teacher's comments

C Teacher's mark

/ 5

 Second Draft

Unit 9 My Vacation in Paris

 Write Your Own.

 student's checklist

Did you
- write a topic sentence? ☐
- use capital letters for proper nouns? ☐
- write a closing sentence? ☐
- check your spelling? ☐
- use punctuation correctly? ☐

Final Draft

Unit 9 My Vacation in Paris

A Write Your Own.

B Teacher's checklist

Did the student:

- write clear and understandable English?
- use simple past tense correctly?
- write strong topic and closing sentences?
- describe feelings adequately?
- spell all words correctly?

D Teacher's comments

C Teacher's mark

/ 5

Unit 10 My Plan for the Baseball Game

A Write Your Own.

B student's checklist

Did you

- write a topic sentence? ☐
- use capital letters for proper nouns? ☐
- write a closing sentence? ☐
- check your spelling? ☐
- use punctuation correctly? ☐

Final Draft

Unit 10 My Plan for the Baseball Game

A Write Your Own.

D Teacher's comments

C Teacher's mark

/ 5

Unit scores

Unit 1:	Unit 2:	Unit 3:	Unit 4:	Unit 5:
Unit 6:	Unit 7:	Unit 8:	Unit 9:	Unit 10:
			TOTAL SCORE:	/50

Teacher's 'end of book' remarks.

Memo!

Memo!